A a

Apple

Ant

B b

Boy

Ball

Cc
Cat
Cup

D d

Dog

Doll

E e

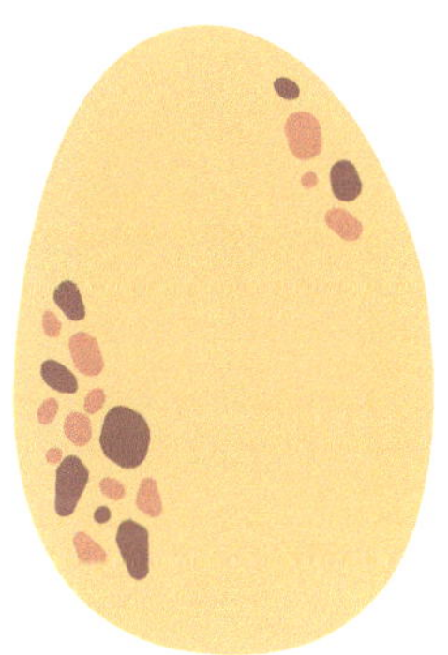

Egg

Elephant

F f

Flower

Fish

Ginger Goat

H h

Hat

Horse

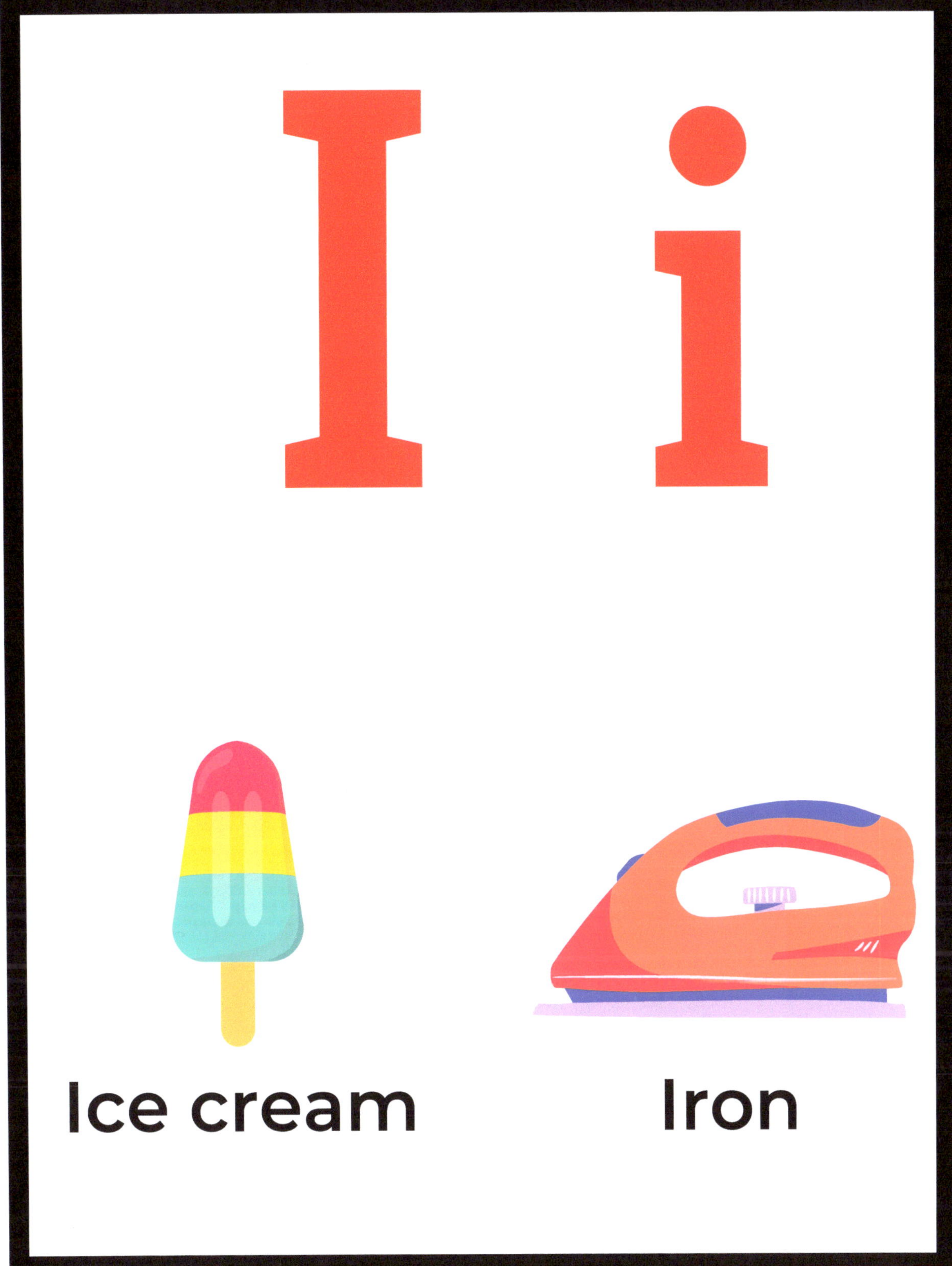
I i
Ice cream
Iron

Jam

Jacket

Kite

Koala

L l
Lion
Ladder

M m

Mango

Mouse

N n

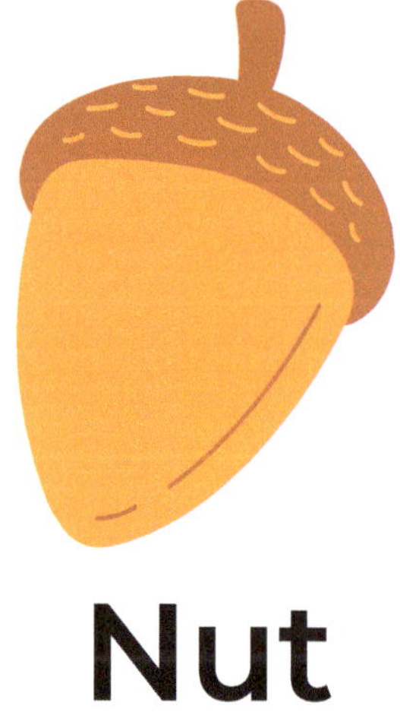

Nut

Nest

Orange

Owl

P p

Peacock

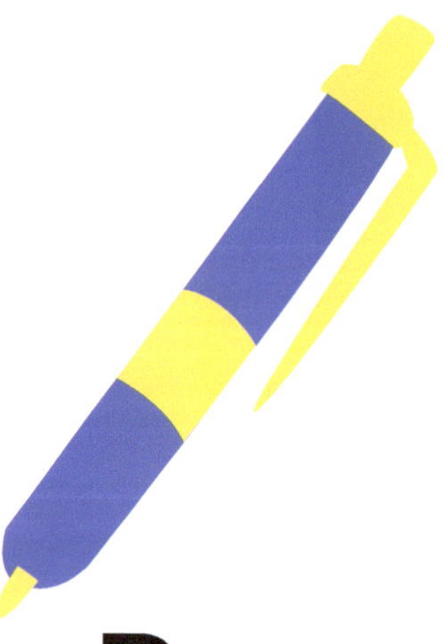

Pen

Q q
Queen
Question

Rr

Rabbit

Rope

Snake

Sun

Tt
Tiger
Table

U u

Umbrella

Unicorn

V v

Vulture

Vase

Wallet

Whale

Xylophone

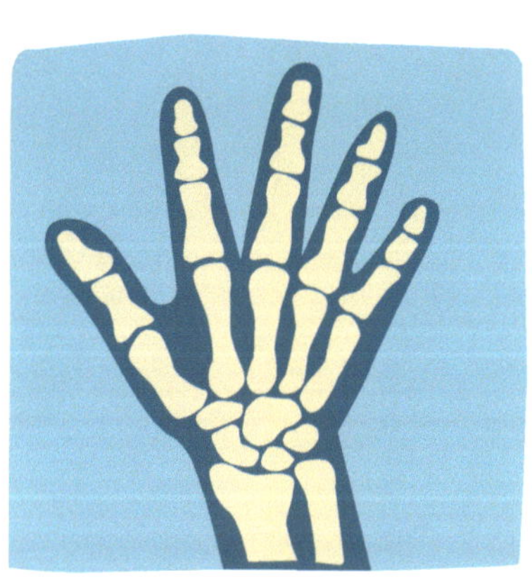

Xray

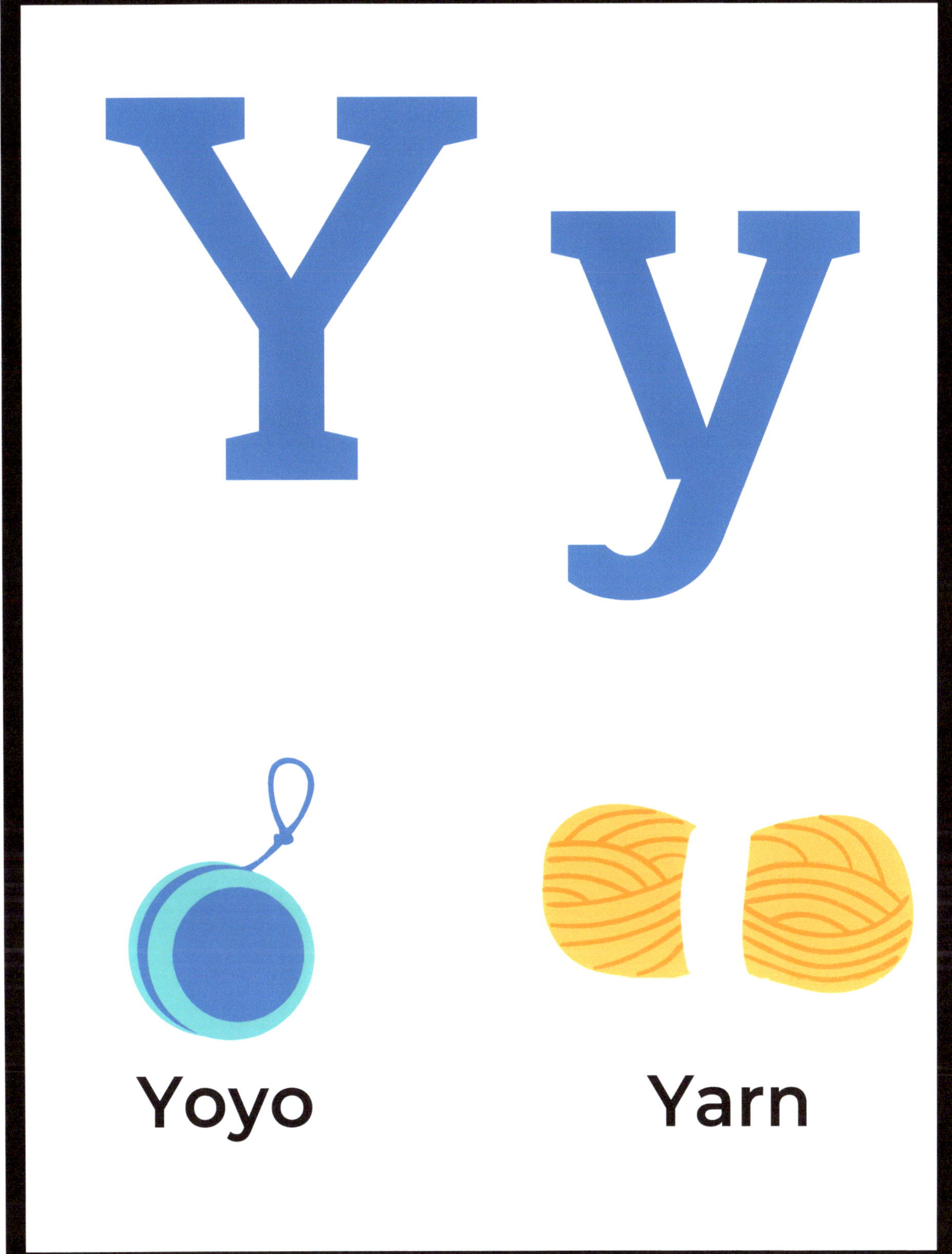
Y y
Yoyo
Yarn

Zebra

Zucchini

www.ingramcontent.com/pod-product-compliance
Lightning Source LLC
LaVergne TN
LVHW071109160826
845679LV00004B/1018

* 9 7 9 8 3 6 6 5 2 7 2 5 5 *